God Made Little Girls Too

WRITTEN BY
Shannon Pfuntner

ILLUSTRATED BY
Lorraine Wright

PUBLISHED BY FIDELI PUBLISHING INC.

© Copyright 2015, Shannon Pfuntner

All Rights Reserved.

No part of this book may be reproduced, stored in a retrieval system, or transmitted by any means, electronic, mechanical, photocopying, recording, or otherwise, without written permission from the author.

ISBN: 978-1-60414-824-4

Dedicated to My Daughters

Harmony Jon Bethany Pfuntner,

Kaelin Jon Elizabeth Pfuntner,

Israel Isabella Keturah Pfuntner

Author's Note

The Lord gave me the precious words in this book after he took my daughter Harmony to heaven. She was born with a rare birth defect. Harmony was beautiful to look upon and our family was saddened by her passing but we knew that she was with Jesus.

One day, I said, "Lord, what do I do now?" As I laid my head on my pillow to sleep that night, he spoke these words into my heart and spirit, "I want you to create a little book for every mother and father to give to their little girls so they will know that God has made them perfect just the way they are with purpose."

I want all of our daughters to know this: you are made perfect by God and no matter what people might say, you are beautiful. Remember, God makes no mistakes.

The book is also for those of you who have lost your daughters, take heart because He created all things perfectly with a perfect design as said in Psalms 139:13-14"

> For you created my inmost being;
> you knit me together in my mother's womb.
> I praise you because I am fearfully and wonderfully made;
> your works are wonderful,
> I know that full well.

I hope that you enjoy every word as you and your daughters read it.

Blessings to your family,
Shannon Pfuntner

God made little girls
white, tan, and black

and all different colors

and the one He has picked
especially for you!

God made little girls to dance and to sing

to Jump and to Swing

God made little girls...

with brown hair,

red hair

and blonde hair too.

And God made

your hair color

just for you!

Israel Isabella Keturah Pfuntner, left, Kaelin Jon Elizabeth Pfuntner, right.

Psalm 139:1-17

O LORD, you have searched me and you know me.
You know when I sit and when I rise;
you perceive my thoughts from afar.
You discern my going out and my lying down;
you are familiar with all my ways.
Before a word is on my tongue
you know it completely, O LORD.
You hem me in-behind and before;
you have laid your hand upon me.
Such knowledge is too wonderful for me,
too lofty for me to attain.
Where can I go from your Spirit?
Where can I flee from your presence?
If I go up to the heavens, you are there;
if I make my bed in the depths, you are there.
If I rise on the wings of the dawn,
if I settle on the far side of the sea,
even there your hand will guide me,

your right hand will hold me fast.
If I say, "Surely the darkness will hide me
and the light become night around me,"
even the darkness will not be dark to you;
the night will shine like the day,
for darkness is as light to you.
For you created my inmost being;
you knit me together in my mother's womb.
I praise you because I am fearfully and wonderfully made;
your works are wonderful, I know that full well.
My frame was not hidden from you
when I was made in the secret place.
When I was woven together in the depths of the earth,
your eyes saw my unformed body.
All the days ordained for me were written in your book
before one of them came to be.
How precious to me are your thoughts, O God!
How vast is the sum of them!

About the Author:

Shannon Pfuntner is the mother of five children and is married to a wonderful man named John.

www.ingramcontent.com/pod-product-compliance
Lightning Source LLC
Chambersburg PA
CBHW061147070526
44584CB00033B/4447